HAMSTERS

Leon Gray

Grolier
an imprint of

www.scholastic.com/librarypublishing

Published 2009 by Grolier
An Imprint of Scholastic Library Publishing
Old Sherman Turnpike
Danbury, Connecticut 06816

For The Brown Reference Group plc
Project Editor: Jolyon Goddard
Picture Researcher: Clare Newman
Designer: Sarah Williams
Managing Editor: Tim Harris

Volume ISBN-13: 978-0-7172-8045-2
Volume ISBN-10: 0-7172-8045-4

**Library of Congress
Cataloging-in-Publication Data**

Nature's children. Set 5.
   p. cm.
  Includes index.
  ISBN-13: 978-0-7172-8084-1
  ISBN-10: 0-7172-8084-5 (set)
  1. Animals--Encyclopedias, Juvenile. I.
Grolier (Firm)
  QL49.N386 2009
  590.3--dc22
                          2008014674

Printed and bound in China

Contents

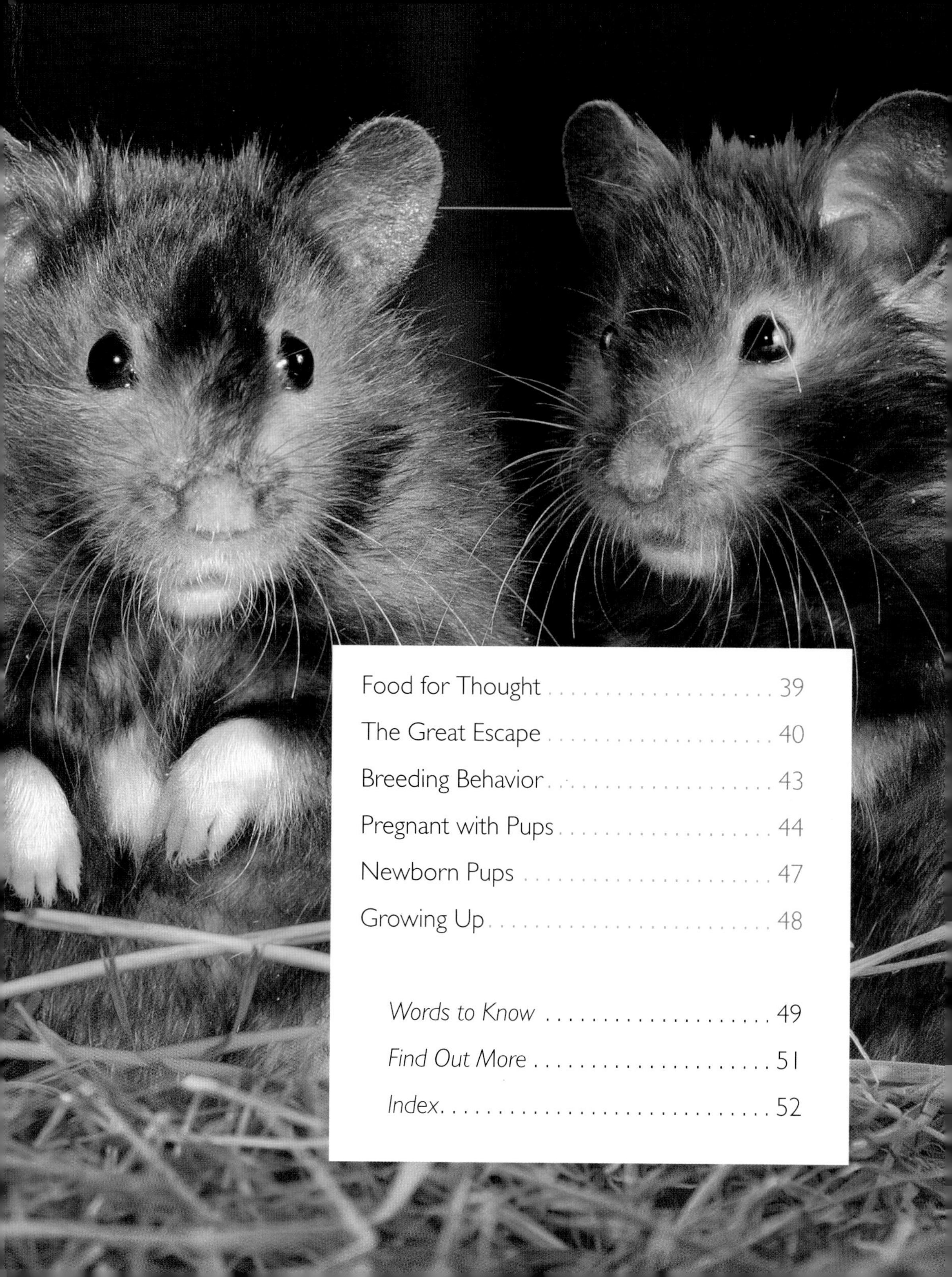

FACT FILE: Hamsters

Class	Mammals (Mammalia)
Order	Rodents (Rodentia)
Family	Mouselike rodents (Muridae)
Genera	Five genera of hamsters and 14 genera of gerbils
Species	Many species of hamsters and gerbils; most pet hamsters are golden hamsters (*Mesocricetus auratus*), and most pet gerbils are Mongolian gerbils (*Meriones auratus*)
World distribution	Pet hamsters and gerbils are found worldwide; wild hamsters and gerbils live in Europe, Asia, and Africa
Habitat	Pets can be kept in a cage or tank with bedding; wild hamsters and gerbils live in grasslands, riverbanks, fields, and deserts
Distinctive physical characteristics	The golden hamster has sleek golden fur, a short tail, and cheek pouches; the Mongolian gerbil has large eyes and ears, with soft fur and a long hairy tail
Habits	Wild hamsters live alone and search for food at night; wild gerbils live in groups
Diet	Pet hamsters and gerbils eat dry food mix, fruit, and vegetables; wild hamsters and gerbils eat seeds, shoots, roots, and insects

Introduction

Hamsters and gerbils make wonderful pets. These small creatures are easy to keep and are very friendly with people. All they need is a clean home, plenty of food and water, and a lot of attention. In fact, hamsters and gerbils are so popular that some people exhibit their pets in shows, just like dogs, cats, and other animals. These pets come in a range of fur colors. Some hamsters even have long hair. In recent years, dwarf and pygmy hamsters and gerbils—the smallest types—have increased in popularity as pets.

Dwarf hamsters, such as this one, grow up to 4 inches (10 cm) long.

The black-bellied hamster lives wild in the grasslands and on riverbanks across Europe and Asia.

6

Hello Hamsters

There are 26 different types, or **species**, of hamsters. The golden, or Syrian, hamster is the species most often kept as a pet. As its name suggests, the golden hamster has soft golden fur. An adult usually measures about 6 inches (12 cm) from its head to the end of its short, stubby tail. Like all hamsters, the golden hamster has distinctive cheek pouches, which it uses to store food.

Other hamster species come in a range of sizes. The smallest is Robovorski's hamster, which is just 2 inches (5 cm) long. The black-bellied hamster is the largest species. These hamsters can measure up to 1 foot (30 cm) long. They have a huge appetite. They can store 100 pounds (45 kg) of food in their **burrows** to help them survive winter.

Gerbil Greetings

Gerbils are popular pets, too. There are 95 species of gerbils, but almost all pet gerbils are Mongolian gerbils, or jirds. An adult Mongolian gerbil measures about 8 inches (20 cm) from its head to the end of its furry tail.

In the wild, Mongolian gerbils roam the deserts of Asia. These animals are hardy—tough enough to survive in the extreme desert climate. Their fur matches the dull color of their sandy **habitat**. But pet gerbils are bred in a wide range of fur colors, including a silvery white, known as argent, gold, and black.

Gerbils often stand upright on their strong back legs to get a better view of their surroundings.

The capybara can weigh more than 500 times the weight of a golden hamster!

Meet the Family

Hamsters and gerbils belong to a large group of mammals called **rodents**. Rodents are found on every continent except Antarctica. Common rodents include mice, rats, chipmunks, guinea pigs, and squirrels. Hamsters and gerbils are closely related to mice and rats—they are all members of a family called the Muridae.

All rodents have sharp front teeth called **incisors**. The animals use their incisors to break open nuts, seeds, and other hard plant matter. Incisors never stop growing. However, rodents wear down their teeth when they gnaw on their tough food.

The largest rodent is the capybara of South America. The females are slightly larger than the males. They grow up to 53 inches (1.3 m) from head to backside and up to 24 inches (62 cm) tall at the shoulders. They can weigh up to 146 pounds (66 kg). Capybaras can live up to 12 years in **captivity**—that's about twice as long as they usually live in the wild.

Pet Relations

Golden hamsters were first taken into captivity in 1930. A zoologist—a scientist who studies animals—named Israel Aharoni collected a female and her babies from the Syrian desert. He bred the hamsters and used them for scientific research. Golden hamsters proved to be popular pets. In fact, most of the pet hamsters in the world are **descendants** of Professor Aharoni's original group of hamsters.

Gerbils share a similar history. The first captive gerbils were bred for research in Japan in about 1935. Roughly 20 years later, a scientist named Victor Schwentker took some of the gerbils back to the United States for his own research. There, gerbils became popular pets. All pet Mongolian gerbils in the United States are descendants of Dr. Schwentker's original gerbils.

Hamsters first came to the United States in the 1930s.

13

Wild golden hamsters
have many predators,
including foxes, eagles,
and snakes.

Survival Stories

Golden hamsters do extremely well as pets, but the future of their wild cousins is less certain. Until Professor Aharoni rediscovered golden hamsters in Syria in 1930, they were thought to be **extinct**. Today, golden hamsters in the wild are endangered. The greatest threat to their survival is the loss of their habitat caused by human activities such as farming.

The future of wild Mongolian gerbils is much brighter. These rodents have few **predators** in their harsh desert habitat, and there is little competition for food. Their survival in the wild is not under threat.

Life in the Desert

Hamsters and gerbils are burrowing rodents. In the wild, they dig their burrows in the sandy soil. During the intense midday heat, these animals remain in their cool burrows. At other times, hamsters and gerbils emerge from their burrows and search for food such as seeds, shoots, and insects. There is little water in the desert, so hamsters and gerbils get almost all of their water from the juicy shoots they eat.

Hamsters and gerbils need to be alert when looking for food. They do not have good eyesight. Instead, they use their sharp sense of smell and well-developed hearing to avoid their enemies. Many animals will attack hamsters and gerbils, including snakes and birds of prey, such as hawks and eagles.

A hamster's whiskers help it feel around in its dark burrow.

Scientists use gerbils and hamsters in experiments to help them try to find cures for many diseases.

Living in the Lab

When hamsters and gerbils were first taken into captivity, they were bred for scientific research. Scientists kept them in laboratories and used them to study a science called **genetics**. This area of science looks at the way in which parents pass on characteristics, such as fur color, eye color, and body size, to their babies. Hamsters and gerbils are ideal for this purpose because they breed quickly and produce a lot of babies.

Hamsters and gerbils have also been used to learn about diseases that affect people, such as heart disease and leprosy. Scientists use the knowledge they gain to save the lives of many other animals and people.

Popular Pets

Rodents have a reputation for carrying diseases. Hamsters and gerbils, however, are very clean and make great pets. They are easy to care for. A hamster can be kept in a cage or glass tank with plenty of clean bedding, such as wood shavings or recycled paper. Gerbils prefer a glass tank lined with straw and a little topsoil. Otherwise, both have the same basic needs—fresh plant food or dry food mix, a good supply of water, and a wooden toy to gnaw on. That will keep their incisors trim. A pet hamster that is treated well should live for two to three years. A pet gerbil may live a little longer—up to four years.

An exercise wheel
keeps a hamster fit.

21

Baby hamsters are born with their eyes closed. They open at about two weeks old.

Living Alone

Hamsters are solitary animals, which means they like to live alone. If you put two adult hamsters in a cage, they will sometimes fight, even to the death. In the wild, a hamster has a **territory**. A territory is an area that a hamster claims as its own. A hamster will defend its territory against other hamsters. A wild hamster marks the boundaries of its territory with its scent to keep away rivals and prevent fights.

Adult hamsters do occasionally meet—to **mate**. Fights still break out, especially if the male is young and inexperienced or the female is not ready to mate. As soon as they've mated, the male and the female part company. The male takes no part in raising young hamsters, or **pups**. When the pups are about three weeks old, the mother pushes them out of the nest. The young hamsters are then left to lead their own solitary life.

Gerbil Groups

Unlike the solitary hamsters, wild Mongolian gerbils live in groups called **colonies**. A colony contains one to three adult males, two to seven adult females, and many younger gerbils. The gerbils build up a store of food in their burrow for winter. When winter comes, they huddle together to keep warm.

If you are going to keep gerbils as pets, it is best to buy a pair. It is always best to get two females, especially those from the same **litter** because they will bond very well. Pairing females from different litters can work out as long as the gerbils meet each other before the age of eight weeks. Unless the owner is ready for a lot more gerbils, it is best to avoid pairing a male and a female.

Different Types

Golden hamsters and Mongolian gerbils are by far the most popular types of pet hamsters and gerbils. They now come in many coat colors, ranging from white and silver to beige, golden, and black—or a mixture of these colors. Their fur can be short or long, satiny or curly.

In recent years, other species of hamsters and gerbils have been bred as pets. Dwarf hamsters are very popular. These types measure between 2 to 4¾ inches (5 to 12 cm) from nose to backside. They include the Chinese hamster and three closely related species—Campbell's dwarf hamster, Roborovski's hamster, and the winter white Russian dwarf hamster.

Small species of gerbils are called pygmy gerbils. They are also becoming popular as pets, especially the northern pygmy gerbil. Another species of gerbil, the fat-tailed gerbil has an almost hairless, clublike tail. These gerbils are very docile and, again, are becoming popular with gerbil fanciers.

Young hamsters play and explore together. By three to four weeks, however, they prefer to live alone.

Choosing a Pet

The best age to buy a pet hamster or gerbil is about five or six weeks old. It is important to check its health before taking it home. Gerbils are naturally alert and active, so pick a bold and curious one. However, the same does not apply for hamsters, which may be a little sleepy depending on the time of day. In both cases, the animal's fur should be clean and well **groomed**, and the ears should stand upright. Gerbils have a long, furry tail, which should be free of bumps and kinks. Avoid taking a pet with streaming eyes and a runny nose, which are signs of a lung disease. Wet fur, bumpy skin, sores, scabs, and bald patches also indicate that the animal is in poor health.

Hamsters are naturally nocturnal—or active at night. Therefore, they may not be fully alert during the day.

A hamster's cage should have bars that are narrowly spaced. That way, the animal will not get its head stuck between the bars.

Happy Homes

A hamster's or gerbil's home should be cleaned
every day, and the bedding must also be changed
regularly. Every month, the home will need a
thorough cleaning with disinfectant. Hamsters
and gerbils quickly catch a chill, so their cage or
tank should be placed in a warm area free from
drafts. Hamsters and gerbils love to run around.
So it is a good idea to put an exercise wheel in
their cage. Some owners let their pet hamsters
and gerbils run loose as long as the area is safe
from predators such as cats.

Handling Tips

A new hamster or gerbil needs some time to settle into its new home. After a few days and some tasty treats, your pet will be ready to be handled. Before picking up a hamster or gerbil, give it plenty of time to sniff your hands so it can become familiar with your scent.

Hamsters and gerbils might bite if they feel frightened or threatened. Never pick up a rodent by its tail and try not to drop your pet. These fragile animals can be easily injured. On some occasions, a hamster or gerbil will try to wriggle away when it is handled. It is best to leave it alone at these times.

Hamsters can pick up infections from humans. It is best to avoid handling your pet when you are ill.

A Campbell's dwarf hamster cleans its face. This species of hamster originates from Russia.

Hamster Habits

Personal hygiene is very important to hamsters and gerbils. They spend a lot of time cleaning their fur, grooming it to a silky sheen with their tongue and paws.

Hamsters and gerbils have an area within their home that is specifically, and only, for relieving themselves. That way, they keep the rest of their home, especially the area where they sleep, as clean as possible. Their area for relieving themselves is usually quite clean and does not normally smell bad. Therefore, the task of cleaning out a pet hamster's or gerbil's home is not too unpleasant!

Hoarding Hamsters

One of the most striking features of a hamster is its baggy cheek pouches, which it uses to collect and store food. In fact, the word hamster comes from the German word *hamstern*, which means "to hoard." The name truly reflects the behavior of this rodent. When a hamster searches for food in the wild, it stores the found items in its cheek pouches. When the pouches are full, the hamster scurries back to its nest. There, the animal uses its front paws to empty all the food into an underground storage chamber. Cheek pouches are also useful for storing pups! A mother hamster might carry her young in them when moving the pups from one place to another.

A hamster's cheek pouches fill up like balloons as it stores food.

Winter white Russian dwarf hamsters, such as this one, live wild in Siberia, Mongolia, and China.

Food for Thought

Hamsters love to hoard food, but they never overeat. Like their gerbil relatives, hamsters need about a tablespoon of food each day. They love to eat cereal grains such as barley, corn, rice, and wheat. Sunflower seeds are ideal as occasional treats, as are fresh vegetables such as carrots, celery, clover, and broccoli. It is important to wash fresh produce, in case it has been sprayed with **pesticides**. Hamsters and gerbils also like fresh fruit. However, citrus fruits, such as oranges, are too acidic for the delicate digestive system of these rodents. Many people who keep hamsters and gerbils prefer to buy dry food mix from a pet store. Dry food mix contains all the nutrients these animals need.

The Great Escape

Hamsters and gerbils move very quickly. It is important to be very careful when opening the door of their cage or when handling them. Make sure when you put your pet back in its cage that the door is closed properly, because it will always find a way out. Unlike a pet dog or cat, a hamster or gerbil does not recognize its name when called. If a pet does escape in your home, the best way to find and catch the animal is to set a trap. Set up a stack of books as a stairway to a bucket of fresh fruit or vegetables. The missing pet will soon come running back for a tasty snack, climb up the book staircase, and fall into the bucket!

Hamsters are naturally curious and will try to get out of their cage given the chance. In the wild, they might range 8 miles (13 km) each evening searching for food.

A pair of northern pygmy gerbils sticks close together. Male and female gerbils grow to the same size.

Breeding Behavior

In the wild, male hamsters go in search of females in the **breeding season**. If the female is not ready to mate, the two hamsters usually fight. If she is ready, they mate. The female hamster then drives the male away. A female hamster makes her own nest and shares it with her litters of pups, which she alone raises.

In Mongolian gerbil colonies, female gerbils usually venture to neighboring colonies to mate before returning to their their own colony. The young are cared for by both their mother and male gerbils in the colony.

Hamsters can mate at four weeks old. Gerbils are old enough to mate a little later, usually around 10 to 12 weeks old. Both hamsters and gerbils are most **fertile** during the summer. In the wild, food is more abundant in summer and the nests are warmer. Both of these factors are important in helping the pups increase their chance of survival.

Pregnant with Pups

Hamsters have one of the shortest pregnancies, or **gestation** periods, of all mammals. Gestation is the time between mating and the birth of the young. For hamsters, this period is just 16 days. The gestation period for gerbils is a little longer, usually about 25 days.

Giving birth puts a lot of strain on the female's body. If you are breeding hamsters or gerbils, it is good idea to give a pregnant hamster or gerbil extra food. In addition, small amounts of dairy products, such as cheese and milk, provide extra nutrients to help ensure that your pet gives birth to healthy pups.

A pregnant Campbell's dwarf hamster prepares for birth. In the wild, the male of this species helps raise the pups, which is unusual for hamsters.

A long-haired white hamster mother keeps her helpless pups together in her nest.

Newborn Pups

A female hamster typically gives birth to seven pups. A female gerbil usually has about five. When each pup is born, it is covered in a skinlike substance, which the mother eats. That way, she regains some of the nutrients she has lost during the gestation period. The newborn pups are blind and deaf, and they do not have fur. They are totally helpless and cannot survive without their mother's milk and the warmth of her body. If your pet hamster has just given birth, it is very important to not touch the pups. Touching the pups will make the mother feel threatened. It may even cause the mother to kill or her own pups. Zoologists—scientists who study animals—are not sure why exactly mother hamsters do that.

Growing Up

Young hamsters and gerbils grow up very quickly. The pups have fur about three days after their birth. After two weeks, the eyes of the hamster pups open. It takes another week for the eyes of the gerbil pups to open.

A female hamster will **nurse** her young for about three weeks. For gerbils, the female nurses her pups for about four weeks. The young hamsters and gerbils then start to eat adult food. Wild young hamsters will then wander off and make their own nests. Wild gerbils often stay together in the colonies in which they were born. The young hamsters and gerbils are then ready to raise their own young.

If you have more than one pet hamster or gerbil and they breed, never release the young outdoors—they will not be able to find the right food or may be eaten by a predator, such as a cat or bird of prey. Instead, make sure they go to a caring owner. With luck, the young rodents will live to three or more years and give their new owners a lot of affection and entertainment.

Words to Know

Breeding season — The time of the year when animals pair up and produce young.

Burrows — Holes dug in the ground for animals to use as homes.

Captivity — When an animal lives in a zoo or someone's home and is not free to roam or live in the wild.

Colonies — Family groups of gerbils.

Descendants — The offspring, their offspring, and so on of an animal or plant.

Extinct — When all of a certain kind of animal or plant are dead and gone forever.

Fertile — Able to have young.

Genetics — A science that looks at the way in which parents pass on characteristics to their offspring.

Gestation — The time it takes for young to develop inside their mother; another word for pregnancy.

Groomed — When an animal's fur is cleaned and tidied.

Habitat	The type of place an animal or plant lives in.
Incisors	The sharp front teeth of mammals.
Litter	A group of baby animals born at the same time to the same mother.
Mate	To come together to produce young.
Nurse	To drink milk from the mother's body.
Pesticides	Chemicals that kill pest animals such as insects.
Predators	Animals that hunt other animals.
Pups	Young hamsters or gerbils.
Rodents	A large group of mammals with front teeth that never stop growing. Hamsters, gerbils, rats, mice, and squirrels are all rodents.
Species	The scientific word for animals of the same kind that breed together.
Territory	An area that an animal defends as its own private space.

Find Out More

Books

Hollimann, P. *My Hamster and Me*. For the Love of Animals Series. Hauppauge, New York: Barron's Educational Series, Inc, 2001.

Landau, E. *Your Pet Gerbil*. True Books. Danbury, Connecticut: Children's Press, 2007.

Web sites

Gerbil Kids @Twinsqueaks
www.twinsqueaks.com/gerbil-kids/
Information about gerbils and activities for children.

Hamster
www.enchantedlearning.com/subjects/mammals/rodent/Hamsterprintout.shtml
Facts about hamsters and a diagram to print.

Index